FANTASTIC FASHION
ORIGAMI

Everyday Style

PowerKiDS
press

CATHERINE ARD

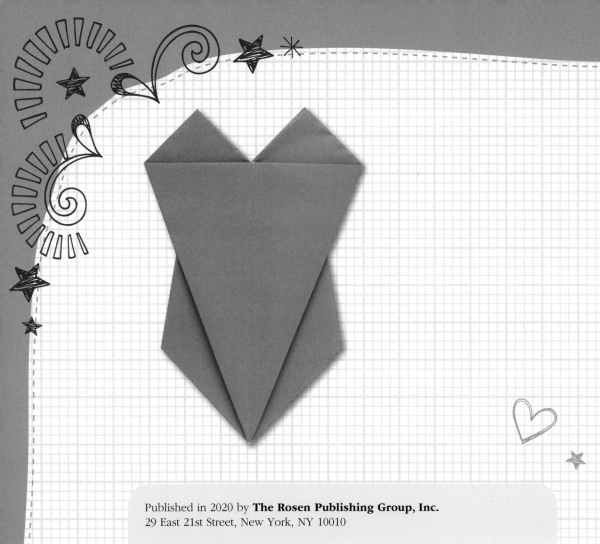

Published in 2020 by **The Rosen Publishing Group, Inc.**
29 East 21st Street, New York, NY 10010

Cataloging-in-Publication Data

Names: Ard, Catherine.
Title: Everyday style / Catherine Ard.
Description: New York : PowerKids Press, 2020. | Series: Fantastic fashion
origami | Includes glossary and index.
Identifiers: ISBN 9781725302822 (pbk.) | ISBN 9781725302846 (library bound)
| ISBN 9781725302839 (6 pack)
Subjects: LCSH: Origami--Juvenile literature. | Paper work--Juvenile literature.
| Fashion--Juvenile literature. | Clothing and dress--Juvenile literature.
Classification: LCC TT872.5 A73 2019 | DDC 736.982--dc23

Copyright © Arcturus Holdings Ltd, 2020

Models and photography by Michael Wiles
Written by Catherine Ard
Designed by Picnic
Edited by Kate Overy and Joe Fullman

Manufactured in the United States of America

CPSIA Compliance Information: Batch CSPK19: For Further Information contact Rosen Publishing,
New York, New York at 1-800-237-9932.

Contents

Introduction

This book shows you how to create a gorgeous collection of mini fashions. All you need for each item is a square of paper, your fingers, and some clever creasing. So, forget sewing and get folding!

Getting started

The paper used in origami is thin, but strong, so that it can be folded many times. You can use ordinary scrap paper, but make sure it's not too thick.

A lot of the clothes in this book are made with the same folds. The ones that appear most are explained on these pages. It's a good idea to master these folds before you start.

Key

When making the clothes, follow this key to find out what the lines, arrows, and symbols mean.

mountain fold ....

direction to move paper ⤵

valley fold – – – – – – – – –

direction to push ▶
or pull paper

step fold (mountain fold and valley fold next to each other)

Mountain fold

To make a mountain fold, fold the paper so that the crease is pointing up at you, like a mountain.

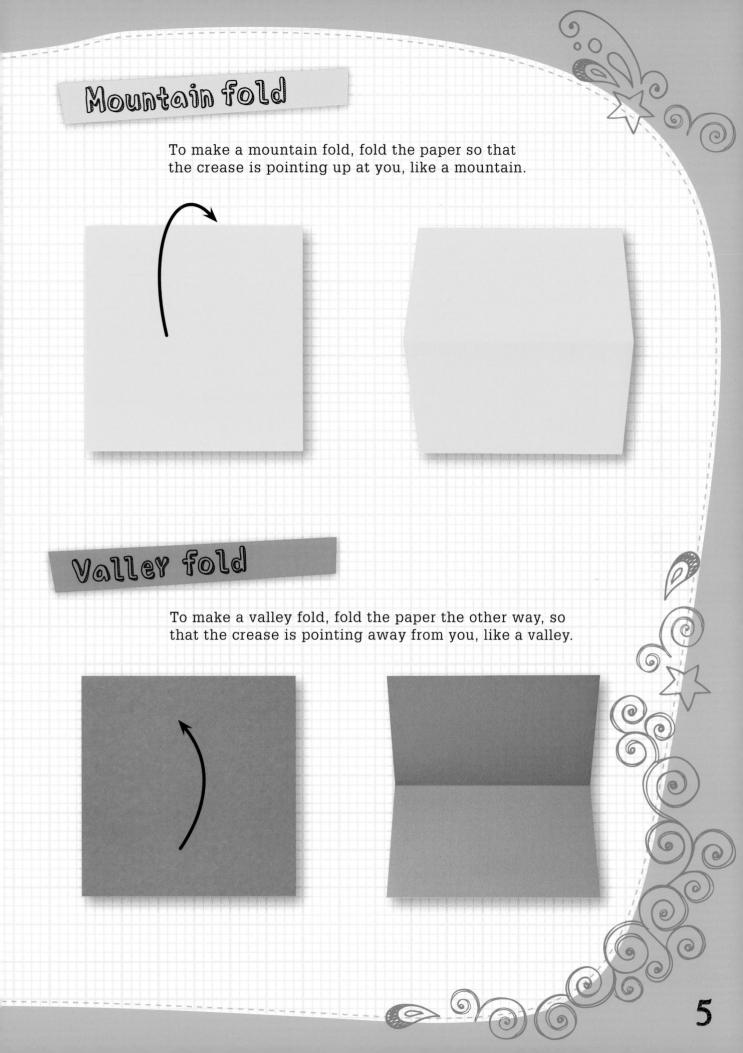

Valley fold

To make a valley fold, fold the paper the other way, so that the crease is pointing away from you, like a valley.

Step fold

The step fold creates a zigzag, or step, in the paper. It is used to divide different parts of a garment, such as the skirt and bodice of a dress.

1 First fold a piece of paper in half, from bottom to top, to make a valley fold.

2 Now unfold.

3 Next make a mountain fold above the valley fold you have just made.

4 Push the mountain fold over the valley fold and press it flat. You now have a step fold.

A step fold like the one here, with the mountain fold above the valley fold, is shown like this.

A step fold with the mountain fold below the valley fold is shown like this.

Pleat fold

Once you have mastered a step fold, making a pleat is easy. In this book, step folds are always horizontal and pleats are vertical. A pleat fold uses some creases that have been made in earlier steps.

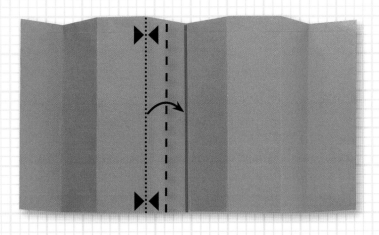

1 To make the first side of a pleat, pinch the crease shown between your fingers. Fold it over to the right until it lines up with the crease indicated. Press it flat to make a valley fold in the paper underneath.

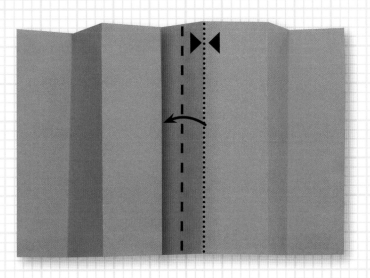

2 Repeat on the other side. Pinch the crease shown and fold it over to the left until it lines up with the crease indicated. Press it flat to make a valley fold underneath.

Hold the paper up and the finished pleat will look like this from the side.

Crop Top

Fold this fun, short shirt and you can rock this cool crop top!

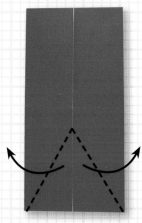

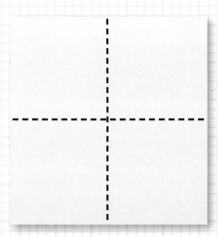

1 Fold the paper top to bottom and unfold. Then fold left to right and unfold.

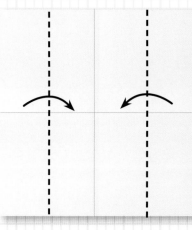

2 Fold the edges in to meet the central crease.

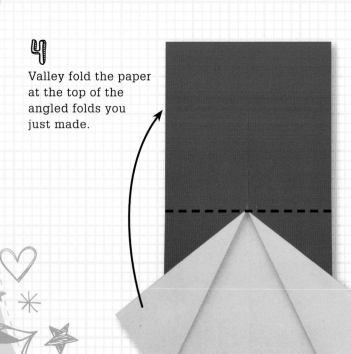

3 Make two angled folds from a finger's width below the middle to the bottom corners. These will be the sleeves.

4 Valley fold the paper at the top of the angled folds you just made.

5 For the collar, make angled creases from the top corners to the middle of the paper.

6

Turn the paper over.

7

Valley fold the corners so that they meet on the central crease.

8

When you have this shape, turn the paper over.

9

Mountain fold the top of the collar as shown.

10

Your crop top is complete. It's cool for the summer and definitely different!

Polo Shirt

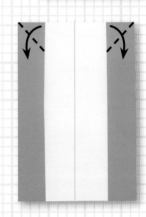

You can't go wrong with this wardrobe staple. You'll have a fashionable shirt after just a few simple folds and creases!

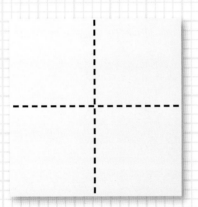

1 Fold the paper top to bottom and unfold. Then fold left to right and unfold.

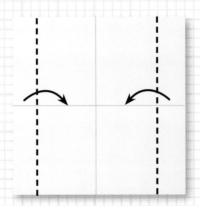

2 Fold in the sides 1 inch (25 mm) from either edge. Mark a faint line to help, if you like.

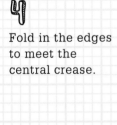

3 Valley fold the top corners to line up with the outside edges.

4 Fold in the edges to meet the central crease.

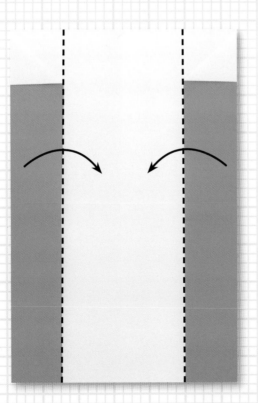

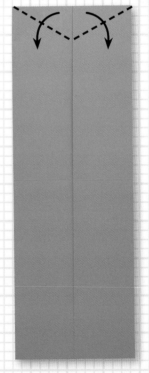

5 To make the collar, make two angled folds that meet in a V in the middle, as shown.

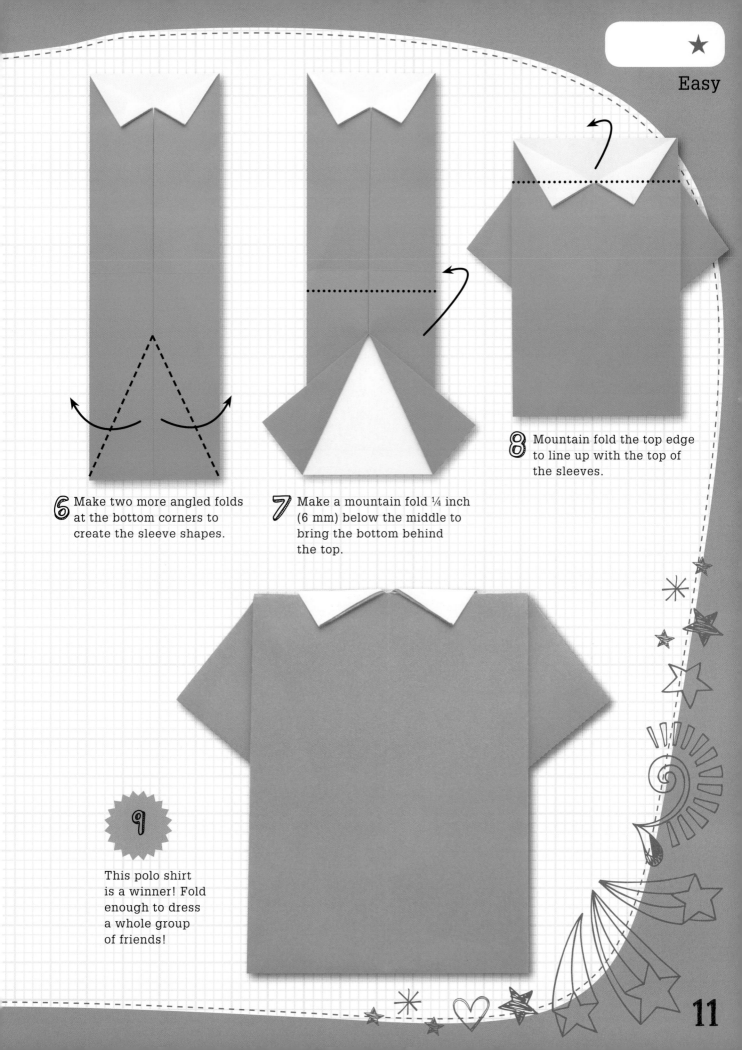

6 Make two more angled folds at the bottom corners to create the sleeve shapes.

7 Make a mountain fold ¼ inch (6 mm) below the middle to bring the bottom behind the top.

8 Mountain fold the top edge to line up with the top of the sleeves.

9 This polo shirt is a winner! Fold enough to dress a whole group of friends!

Smock Top

Make a swinging smock top with plenty of Sixties style. Pick a strong shade to make the white neck and border really pop!

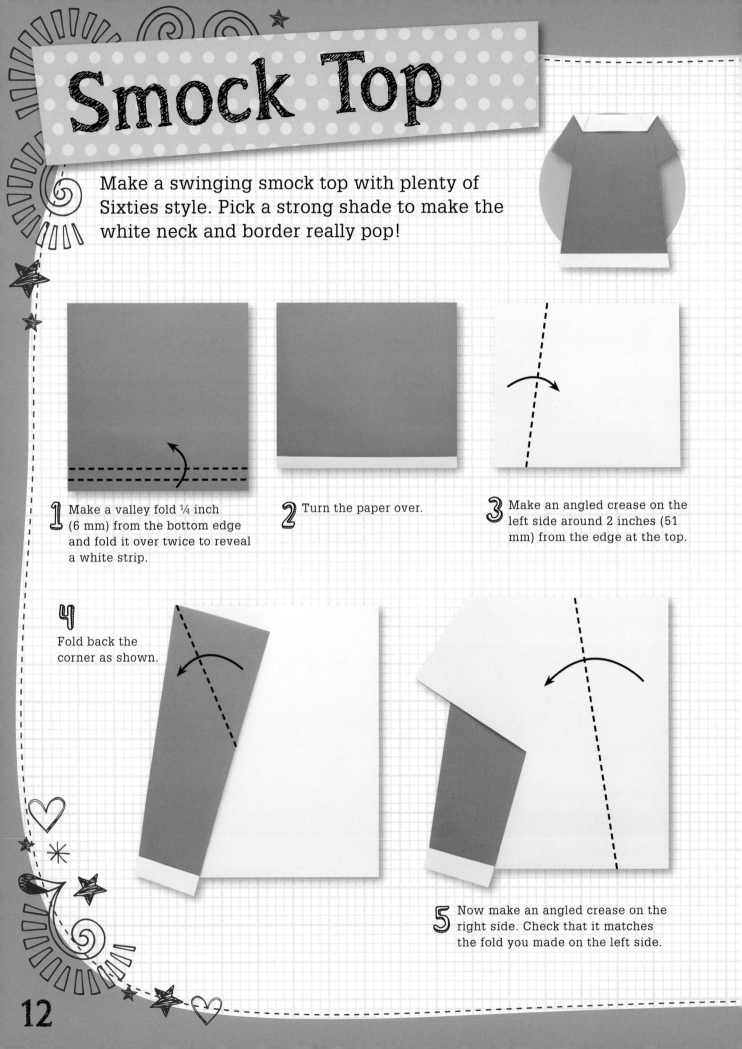

1 Make a valley fold ¼ inch (6 mm) from the bottom edge and fold it over twice to reveal a white strip.

2 Turn the paper over.

3 Make an angled crease on the left side around 2 inches (51 mm) from the edge at the top.

4 Fold back the corner as shown.

5 Now make an angled crease on the right side. Check that it matches the fold you made on the left side.

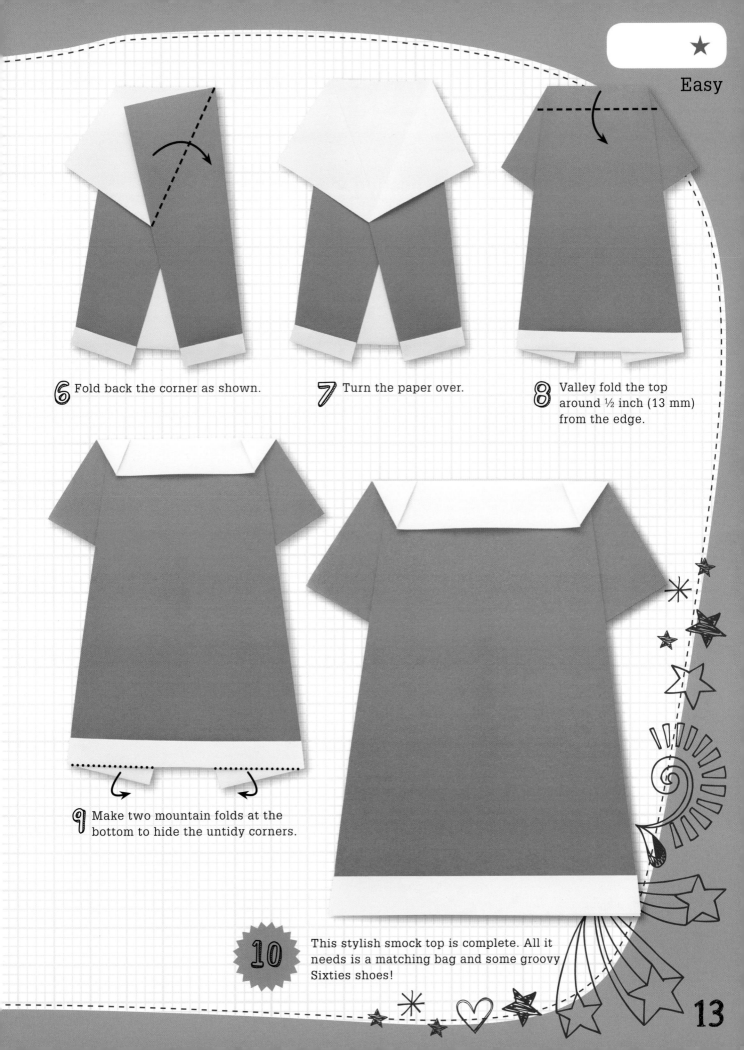

6 Fold back the corner as shown.

7 Turn the paper over.

8 Valley fold the top around ½ inch (13 mm) from the edge.

9 Make two mountain folds at the bottom to hide the untidy corners.

10 This stylish smock top is complete. All it needs is a matching bag and some groovy Sixties shoes!

Sailor Top

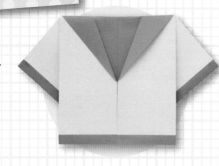

Ahoy there! This stylish boating top will add some fun to your paper fashions. Choose a bright ocean blue and set sail for the high seas!

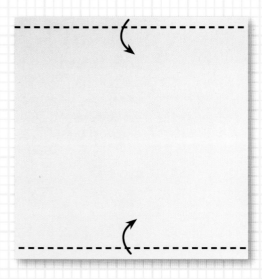

1 Valley fold a narrow section on the top and bottom edges.

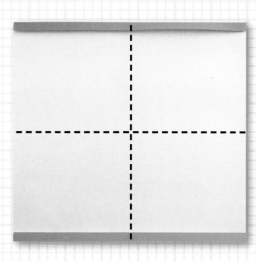

2 Fold the paper in half from top to bottom and unfold. Then fold it from left to right and unfold. Turn the paper over.

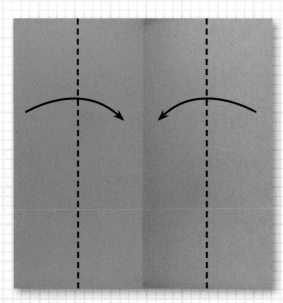

3 Fold the edges in to meet the central crease.

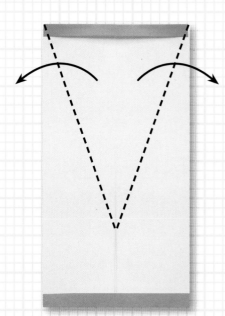

4 Make two angled folds from the top corners that meet in a V around 1½ inches (38 mm) below the middle. This will shape the sleeves and collar.

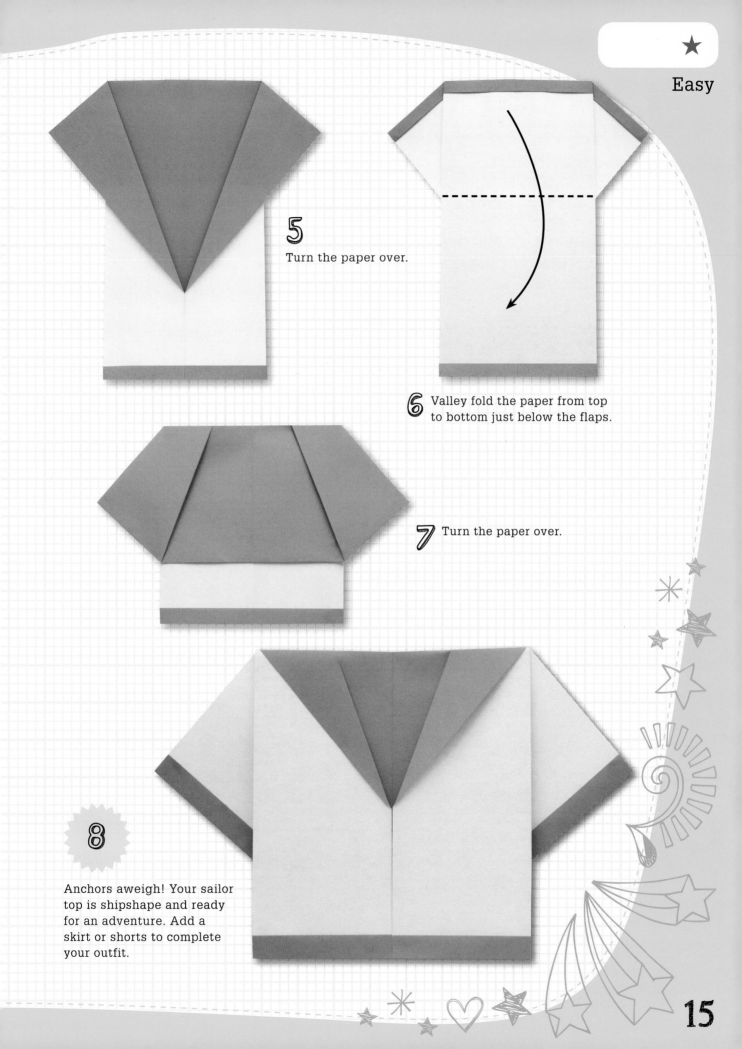

5 Turn the paper over.

6 Valley fold the paper from top to bottom just below the flaps.

7 Turn the paper over.

8 Anchors aweigh! Your sailor top is shipshape and ready for an adventure. Add a skirt or shorts to complete your outfit.

T-shirt and Shorts

Fold a pair of simple shorts and a comfy T-shirt. It's the perfect outfit for hot summer days. Coordinate the top and shorts, or mix and match different papers.

T-SHIRT

1 Fold the paper from left to right and unfold. Then fold it top to bottom and unfold.

2 Fold in the edges to meet the central crease.

3 Valley fold a narrow section on both edges so a white strip is showing.

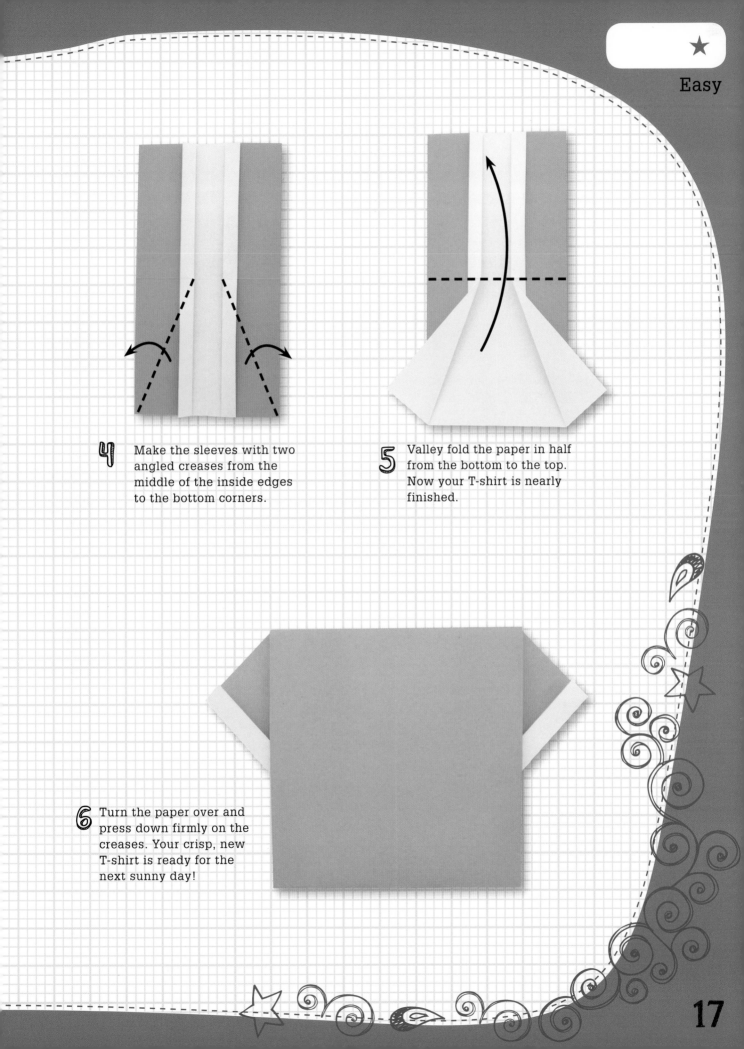

4 Make the sleeves with two angled creases from the middle of the inside edges to the bottom corners.

5 Valley fold the paper in half from the bottom to the top. Now your T-shirt is nearly finished.

6 Turn the paper over and press down firmly on the creases. Your crisp, new T-shirt is ready for the next sunny day!

SHORTS

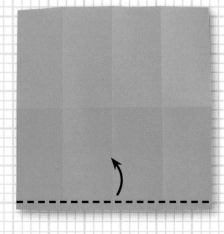

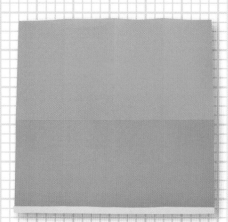

1 Follow steps 1 and 2 from the T-shirt instructions, then unfold the paper. Fold the bottom edge in, as shown.

2 Turn the paper over.

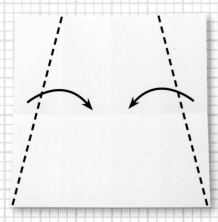

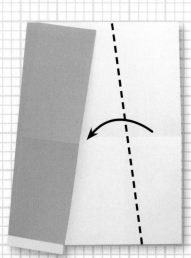

3 Make angled creases from the bottom corners to the first crease along the top edge on either side.

4 Fold in one side, pressing down firmly. Repeat on the other side. These will be the legs.

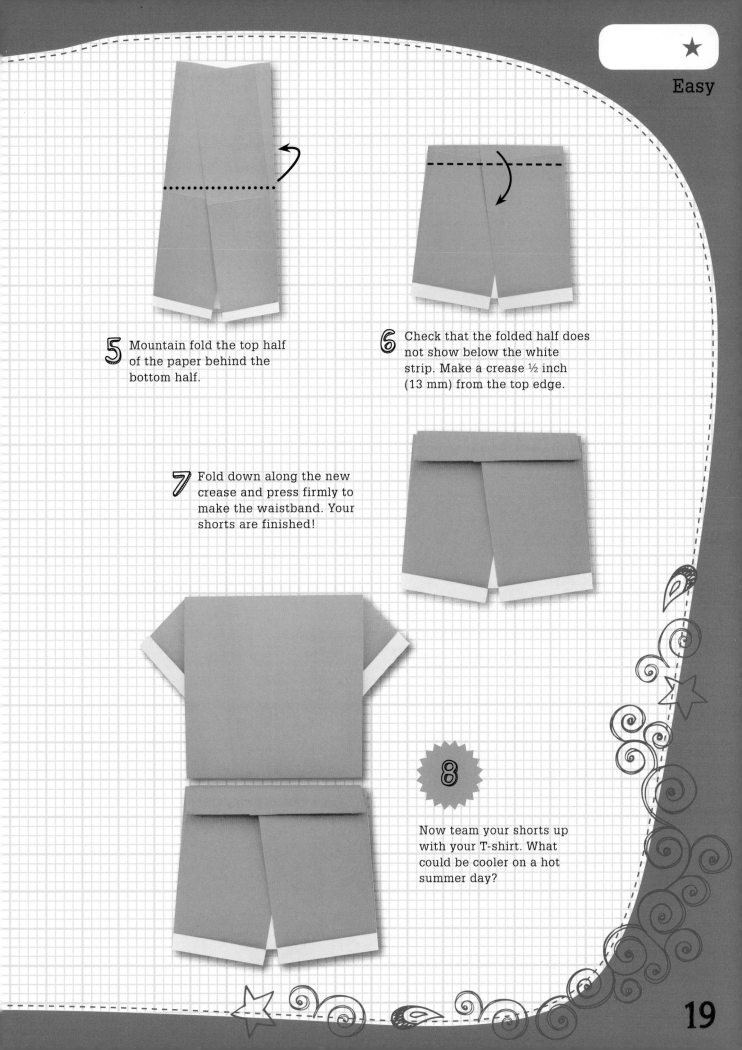

5 Mountain fold the top half of the paper behind the bottom half.

6 Check that the folded half does not show below the white strip. Make a crease ½ inch (13 mm) from the top edge.

7 Fold down along the new crease and press firmly to make the waistband. Your shorts are finished!

8 Now team your shorts up with your T-shirt. What could be cooler on a hot summer day?

Swimsuit

Make a splash on sunny days with a cute swimsuit that's easy to fold. Blend in at the beach in ocean blue, or stand out at the pool with a bright shade.

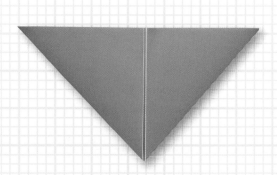

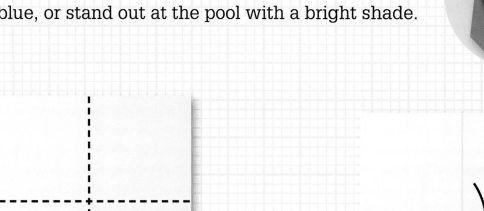

1 Fold the paper in half from top to bottom and unfold. Then fold from left to right and unfold.

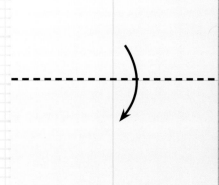

2 Fold the paper in half from top to bottom once more.

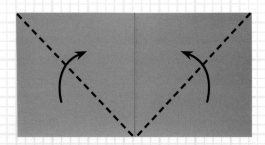

3 Fold the bottom corners up to meet in the middle of the top edge.

4 You should now have a triangle. Unfold the last two folds.

20

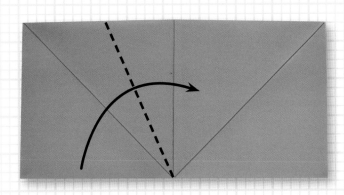

5 Fold the left side over so the bottom edge meets the diagonal crease on the opposite side.

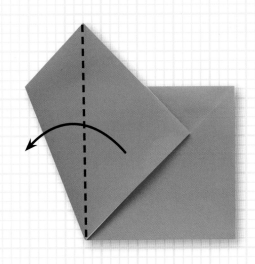

6 Valley fold the paper along the original fold to make a triangle.

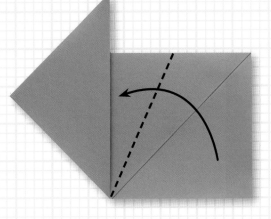

7 Repeat steps 5 and 6 on the other side. You can open up the paper to check that the bottom edge meets the diagonal crease on the opposite side.

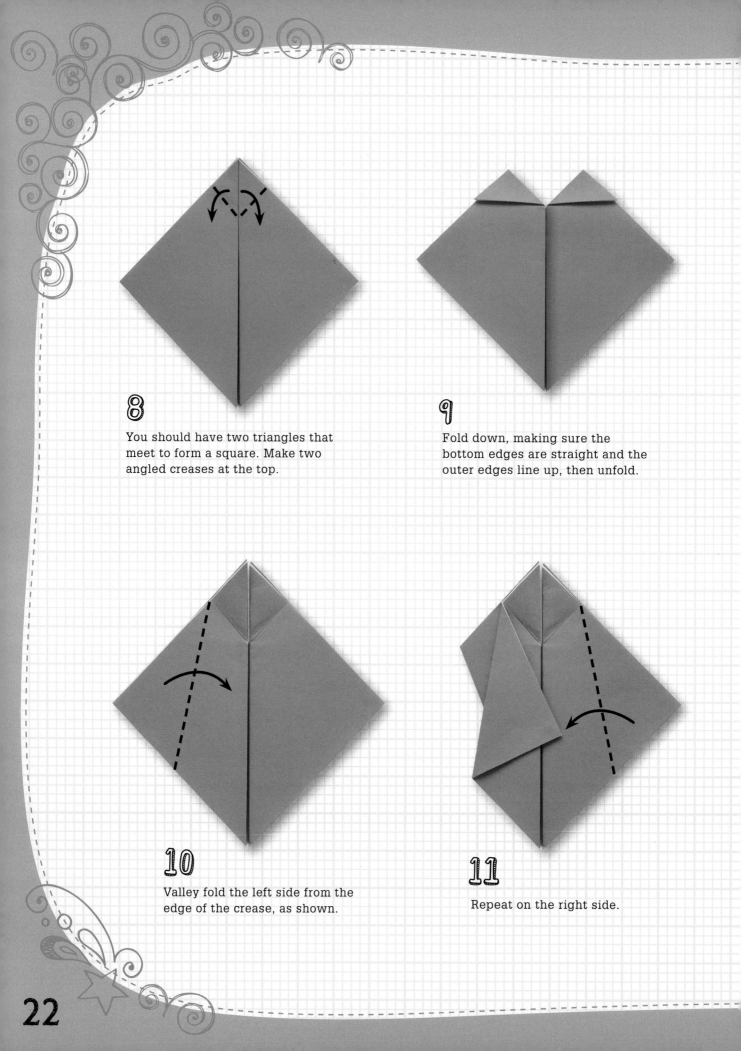

8

You should have two triangles that meet to form a square. Make two angled creases at the top.

9

Fold down, making sure the bottom edges are straight and the outer edges line up, then unfold.

10

Valley fold the left side from the edge of the crease, as shown.

11

Repeat on the right side.

12 Your paper should look like this. Turn the paper over.

13 Mountain fold the top corners along the creases that you made before. Press down firmly.

14 Your strapless swimsuit is ready for a dip. Time to grab the sunscreen and hit the beach!

Pleated Skirt

When it comes to paper fashions, pleats are totally neat, so get folding to make an easy, pleated skirt that's stylish, too!

1 Make a fold around ¼ inch (6 mm) from the top edge so a white strip is showing.

2 Turn the paper over, keeping the white strip at the top.

3 Fold the paper in half from left to right.

4 Crease firmly, then unfold the paper again.

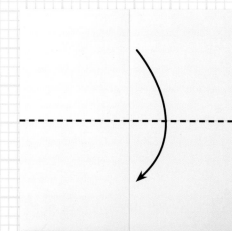

5 Fold the paper in half from top to bottom.

6 Fold the edges in to meet the central crease.

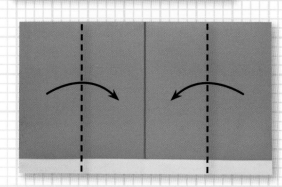

7 Repeat step 6, folding the edges in to meet the central crease.

8 Your paper should look like this. Unfold the paper, keeping the white strip at the bottom.

9 Turn the paper over.

10 Now make the first pleat. Take the third crease from the left to meet the central crease. Press it flat.

11 Repeat step 10 on the other side, taking the third crease from the right to meet the central crease. Press it flat.

12 You should now have a pleat down the middle of the paper.

It should look like this from the side. Turn the paper over.

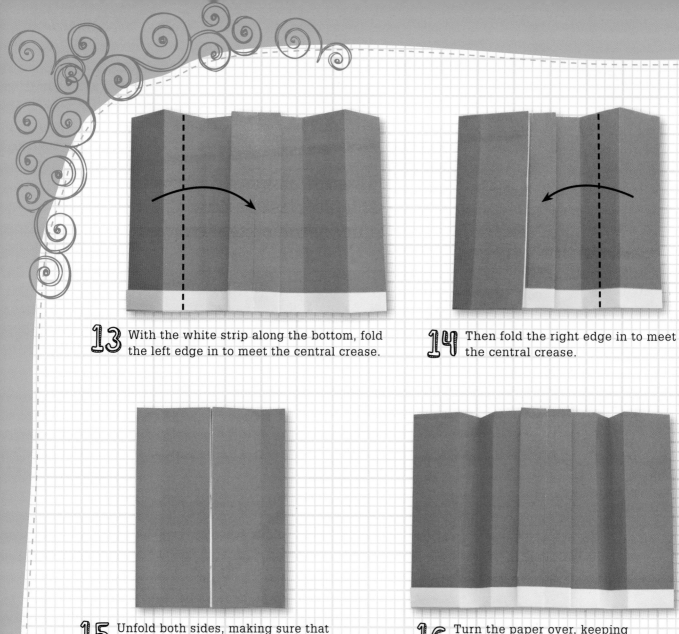

13 With the white strip along the bottom, fold the left edge in to meet the central crease.

14 Then fold the right edge in to meet the central crease.

15 Unfold both sides, making sure that the pleat you made is still in place.

16 Turn the paper over, keeping the white strip at the bottom.

17

Now make another pleat. Take the second crease from the left and fold it over along the third crease.

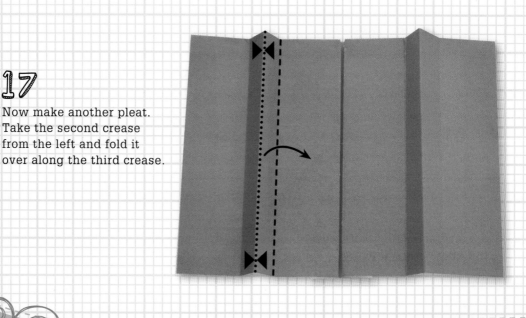

18 Repeat step 17 on the other side, taking the second crease from the right and folding it over along the third crease.

19 Make a valley fold from the first crease on the top edge to the bottom corner.

20 Make a matching fold on the other side to create the flared shape of the skirt.

21 Fold down the top ½ inch (13 mm) of the skirt to hide the open edges. Your skirt is nearly ready.

22 Press down firmly along the top to crease the pleated layers, then turn the paper over.

23 Ta-da! One neatly pleated skirt, complete with a pretty band, ready to swing into action!

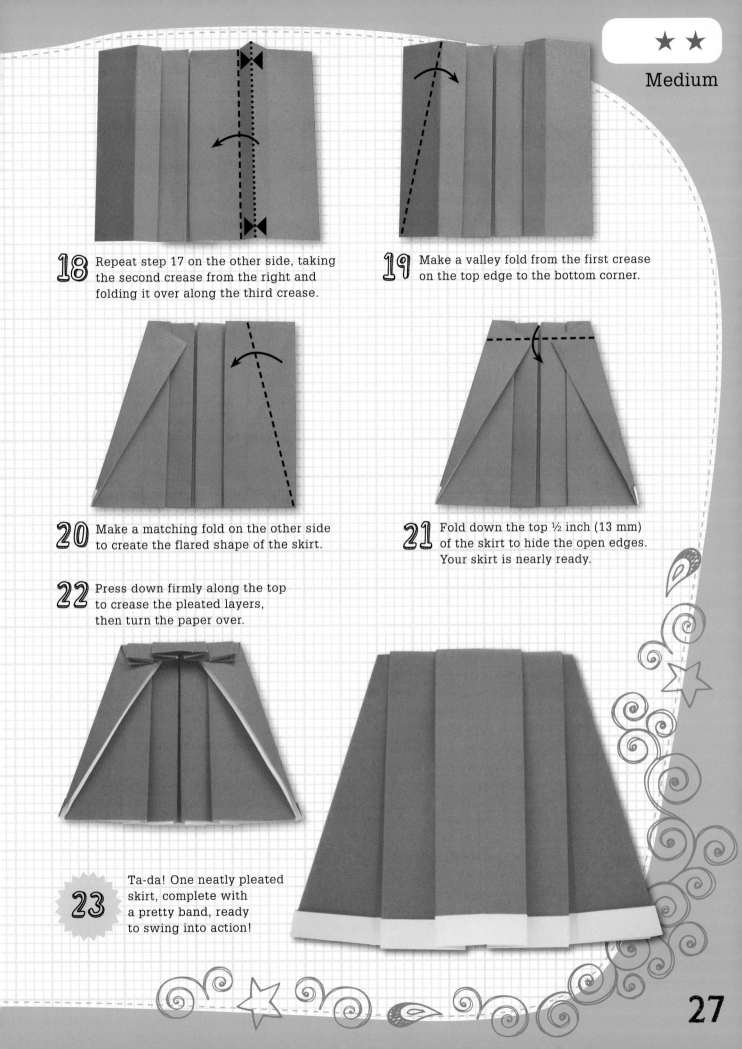

Jumper

This pretty, everyday jumper dress is a must for a fun summer wardrobe. Pair it with a T-shirt for a polished look.

1. Fold the paper in half from top to bottom and unfold. Then fold from left to right and unfold.

2. Fold the edges in to meet the central crease.

3. Unfold the paper.

4. Fold in both sides about ½ inch (13 mm) from the edge.

5. Mountain fold the sides along the creases that you made earlier.

6. Make a new crease about 1 inch (25 mm) from the top edge.

7. Fold down the paper and crease firmly.

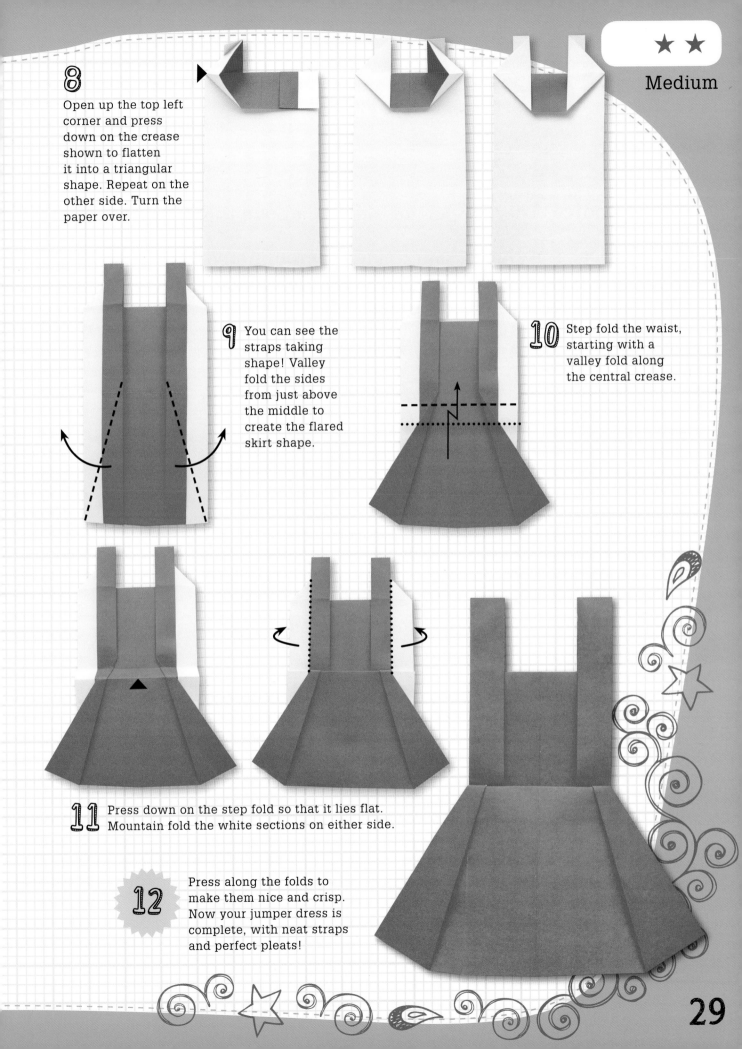

8 Open up the top left corner and press down on the crease shown to flatten it into a triangular shape. Repeat on the other side. Turn the paper over.

9 You can see the straps taking shape! Valley fold the sides from just above the middle to create the flared skirt shape.

10 Step fold the waist, starting with a valley fold along the central crease.

11 Press down on the step fold so that it lies flat. Mountain fold the white sections on either side.

12 Press along the folds to make them nice and crisp. Now your jumper dress is complete, with neat straps and perfect pleats!

29

# Glossary

bodice The top part of a dress, above the waist.

crease A line or mark made by folding something, such as a piece of paper. Also, to fold something so that a crease is formed.

garment Any item of clothing.

horizontal Parallel to the horizon, at right angles to the vertical.

mountain fold A fold where the crease points up at you, like a mountain.

Sixties The 1960s.

smock A loose piece of clothing.

step fold A fold that creates a zigzag, or step, in the paper.

valley fold A fold where the crease points away from you, like a valley.

vertical Straight up and down.

Further Information

Books

George, Lauren Delaney. *L. Delaney's All Dolled Up: Creating a Paper Fashion Wardrobe for Paper Dolls.* Mineola, NY: Dover Publications, 2017.

Song, Sok. *Everyday Origami: A Foldable Fashion Guide.* North Mankato, MN: Capstone Press, 2016.

Song, Sok. *Origami Outfits: A Foldable Fashion Guide.* North Mankato, MN: Capstone Press, 2016.

Websites

en.origami-club.com/clothes/index.html
This website shows you how to make all kinds of origami clothes, from T-shirts to wedding dresses.

www.origami-make.org/howto-origami-kids.php
This website has instructions for making all sorts of origami creations, including shirts, pants, and a tote bag!

Publisher's note to educators and parents: Our editors have carefully reviewed these websites to ensure that they are suitable for students. Many websites change frequently, however, and we cannot guarantee that a site's future contents will continue to meet our high standards of quality and educational value. Be advised that students should be closely supervised whenever they access the Internet.

Index